IN THE MASS

The Life of Christ in the Mass

by
Saint Vincent Ferrer, OP

Translated by
Fr. Albert Judy, OP

TAN Books
Gastonia, North Carolina

English translation copyright © 2024 TAN Books

All rights reserved. With the exception of short excerpts used in critical review, no part of this work may be reproduced, transmitted, or stored in any form whatsoever, without the prior written permission of the publisher. Creation, exploitation, and distribution of any unauthorized editions of this work, in any format in existence now or in the future—including but not limited to text, audio, and video—is prohibited without the prior written permission of the publisher.

Translated by Fr. Albert Judy, OP

Cover design by Jordan Avery

Front Cover image: The Mass of Saint Gregory, after 1720 original by Pietro Ligari (1686-1752), 1864 (oil on canvas). Photographed by Paolo Manusardi. © Veneranda Biblioteca Ambrosiana / Mondadori Portfolio /Bridgeman Images.

Back Cover Image: St. Vincent Ferrer by Juan de Juanes, 1445-1450. Oil on panel. Photographed by Web Gallery of Art. Wikimedia Commons.

ISBN: 978-1-5051-3247-2
Kindle ISBN: 978-1-5051-3248-9
ePUB ISBN: 978-1-5051-3249-6

Published in the United States by
TAN Books
PO Box 269
Gastonia, NC 28053
www.TANBooks.com

Printed in India

"Whatever you do, think not of yourself, but of God."

—Saint Vincent Ferrer, OP

Every Christian ought to believe what the Master, Jesus, on Holy Thursday ordained and instituted the holy sacrament of the Mass, to the holy apostles present, and He commanded them that they were to do the same with great reverence and perpetual memorial, according to what St. Luke says (see Luke 22:19), and St. Paul to the Corinthians, "Do this in memory of me" (1 Cor. 11:24)—namely, you should want to recall and devoutly remember, by hearing Mass, the entire blessed life of Jesus Christ. For this reason, the priest, when elevating the chalice, says, "As often as you shall do these actions, do this in memory of Me." He does not say: "In memory of My passion," but "in My memory," signifying that the Mass comprehends not only the sacred death of Jesus Christ, but also, quietly [tacite], His blessed life, beginning from His incarnation up to the holy Ascension.

Someone might say, "This command was only given to and imposed upon priests and not laypeople." I reply that this command was also given to the laity. To the priests it was ordained that they remember the holy life of Jesus Christ by devoutly celebrating Mass; to the laity, however, by devoutly hearing, attentively listening, and contemplating.

And I find that the Son of God, descending from heaven and assuming human flesh in the virginal womb of the Most Holy Virgin Mary, up to the day on which He ascended to heaven, did thirty principal deeds, which are comprehended and reprised in the Mass. And they are the following:

1. The first work which our Master and Savior Jesus Christ did for us in this world was His sublime and wonderful incarnation when, descending from heaven, He placed Himself in the bosom of the Virgin Mary, by which He put on our vesture, that is our humanity; for the divinity was hidden under the humanity. And this wonderful work is symbolized and represented in the Solemn Mass when the priest enters the sacristy, signifying the entry of the Son of God into the bosom of the Virgin Mary, where He was clothed with our humanity.

Here, the devout Christian ought to contemplate three things: first, that just as in the sacristy there are relics, jewels, and other ecclesiastical decorations, so in this glorious sacristy—that is, in the Virginal womb, there were relics—namely, the power of God the Father working, wisdom and the person of God the Son incarnating Himself, and the grace of the Holy Spirit informing. There were jewels—namely, grace and virtues, for in the Virgin Mary dwells the fullness of grace and the virtues; and ornaments with which our high priest is about to celebrate Mass, on Good Friday, on the altar of the True Cross, in the sacred and sanctified Body of Jesus Christ, from the purest and most chaste blood of the Virgin Mary formed and incarnated.

Second is that, when the priest is vested in the sacristy, no layperson sees him; but they believe that he is vested and they hope that he will come forward shortly.

For which it must be noted that when our high priest Jesus Christ vested Himself in the virginal womb of the Virgin Mary, no one from the Jewish people saw Him or knew Him; in the same way that His incarnation was hidden and kept secret, the believers however believed and hoped that He would vest Himself, that is, be incarnated and born of the Virgin, just as it had been prophesied by many prophets.

Third is that the priest puts on seven vestments in the sacristy—namely, the cassock, if he is a simple priest—a rochet if is he is a bishop, a scapular if he is a monk;—amice, alb, cincture, maniple, stole, and chasuble. So, our great high priest vested Himself in the womb of the Virgin Mary, who is called a sacristy, with seven vestments—namely, the seven gifts of the Holy Spirit, by which the most sacred Body of Jesus Christ is vested and dressed (Is. 11:2–3). This is the first work in the symbolism of the Mass.

2. The second work which our Savior Jesus did was when, on the night of His birth, God and man He came out from the virginal womb and revealed Himself to the whole world, and the night, which had been dark, is illuminated like the day. And He wished to be born before Joseph and Mary, and placed in the middle of two animals, the ass and the ox. And a multitude of angels were singing, "Glory to God in the highest!" And the shepherds worshiped.

Secretly, He remained in the glorious sacristy—that is, in the Virgin Mary, after His birth, openly and publicly

He declared Himself. This is symbolized when the priest comes out from the sacristy. The deacon represents the Virgin Mary; the subdeacon, St. Joseph; the two acolytes, the ox and the ass. The light which they carry signifies the brightness which showed forth at the birth of our Savior Jesus Christ. The priests who with candles and with a loud voice sing, "Glory to the Father . . ." when the priest goes out from the sacristy, they represent the multitude of angels singing: "Glory is given to God." The cymbals sound and the bells ring, which signifies the great joy of the shepherds when they were celebrating the birth of our Savior and high priest with the sound of flutes [tibiarum]. When he exits from the sacristy, dressed in gleaming vestments, the priest symbolizes the purity of Jesus Christ, Who, pure and shining, remained without the stain of sin.

3. The third wonderful work which Jesus Christ did was when He willed to be circumcised on the eighth day after His nativity. For original sin circumcision happened, for which in no way was Jesus Christ obliged since He was without any stain of sin; but accepting it He taught us a great example of humility, wishing to appear a sinner and in the likeness of sin.

And this the priest symbolizes when, making a profound bow, he confesses that he is a sinner, saying, "I confess to almighty God." Although the priest is sacramentally absolved, he is nevertheless bound to declare himself a sinner, even if he were holier than John the Baptist, to demonstrate and signify that Jesus Christ,

Who is the beginning and fullness of all sanctity and perfection, wished to appear a sinner, subjecting Himself to the law of circumcision so that He might put an end to it and complete it; or signifying the mystical Body of the Church and all of mankind.

4. The fourth work which He did was when He summoned the three kings from the East, led by a star, which led them up to the manger of the ox and ass, in the middle of which they adored and confessed Him to be God and Lord of the universe, offering Him gold, frankincense, and myrrh.

This is symbolized when the priest, after the confession, ascends the altar and kisses it, profoundly bowing his head saying, "Take away from us, O Lord, we beseech You, all our iniquities that we may enter with pure minds into the Holy of Holies."[1] And just as three kings brought three gifts, the priest offers, by bowing himself, the incense of devout prayer, the gold of adoration with great reverence, and the bitter myrrh, signing himself with the sign of the Holy Cross in memory of the sorrowful and bitter passion of Jesus Christ.

5. The fifth work which Jesus Christ did in this world was when He wished to be presented in the temple. His glorious Mother brought Him there and presented Him, and there were present Simeon and that holy widow, Anna, praising God.

This the priest symbolizes when he comes to the side of the altar, receives the missal and reads the Entrance Antiphon [Introit] of the Mass. The deacon, subdeacon, and assistant symbolize the glorious Simeon and the prophetess, Anna. The acolytes and the others, who should not approach the altar, symbolize the Virgin Mary and St. Joseph, and the other ancients and parents, who were standing at a distance, hearing and devoutly paying attention. Truly, the Virgin Mary was entirely worthy that she would approach the altar, but she chose not to, to give an example to the laity who also, as holy and justified, ought not ascend to the altar unless because of an urgent necessity, otherwise not without sin [*non sine damno*]. When the holy man Simeon received the glorious Son of God, he sang four verses (Luke 2:29–32), signifying the four actions which the priest does—namely, the reading of the Introit; the *Kyrie eleison*, which is the same as imploring the mercy of God the Father for himself and others; the Glory to God (the *Gloria*); and the Prayer (the Collect).

6. The sixth work which Our Lord Jesus Christ did in this world was when He fled from the promised land to the land of Egypt, yielding the place to the fury of Herod. And here He remained with His glorious Mother and St. Joseph for seven years.

And this is represented in a Solemn Mass when the subdeacon, with one acolyte, goes to read the Epistle, the priest remaining at the altar with another [acolyte] and the deacon; and then they take themselves from the altar and are seated; and sitting they do seven things, which represent the seven years when Jesus Christ remained in Egypt: first, the Epistle is read; second, the

Responsory; third, the Alleluia (a Hebrew word which means "We praise God"); fourth, a Sequence [prosa]; fifth, a blessing is given to the deacon—he performs the last act standing, signifying that in the seventh year, Jesus Christ returned to His own land.

7. The seventh work which He did in this world was when, having returned from Egypt into the promised land after the death of Herod, led by His Mother and St. Joseph into the temple of Jerusalem, and there He stayed. And on the third day, His Mother and Joseph discovered Him in the middle of the teachers, listening to them and asking questions.

And the priest represents this when, rising from his seat, goes to the altar and with devout attention listens to the singing of the Gospel, signifying that in the temple Jesus Christ listened to the Jews, and He, having been prudently questioned, was instructing them in the faith of the Messiah. And so, the Gospel ended, the priest intones the *Credo*, "I believe in one God."

8. The eighth work which our Savior Jesus Christ did in this world was that when He was found by His Mother and St. Joseph in the temple, so great was their joy that they were not able to keep from tears; which Jesus Christ seeing, out of humility and love, He left the teachers and came with them to Nazareth where, that He might console them of the sadness which they had had at His omission, He served them, according to the Gospel which says: "He was subject to them" (Luke 2:51).

And this humble service the priest symbolizes when, having said the Creed, he turns to the people saying, "The Lord be with you"; and then he arranges [disponit] the host and chalice, and the other things pertaining to the holy sacrifice, symbolizing the deference of Jesus Christ toward the Virgin Mary and St. Joseph; as it is said by St. Paul and St. Matthew, "the Son of man is not come to be ministered unto, but to minister" (Matt. 20:28).

9. The ninth work which He did in this world was, when thirty years old, He left Nazareth where He was serving His Mother and St. Joseph, and in many ways: for with the other boys He used to go to the spring, which was a long way from Nazareth, just as the monastery of the Çaydia is from the town of Valencia. Of this service the Master of Church History (Peter Comestor, died 1178) makes explicit mention. Also, He would help St. Joseph in his carpentry work, just as Matthew says, (in ch. 13:55 and Mark ch. 6:3) and according to the Gloss by St. Nicholas of Lyra on these Gospels. And after He had completed thirty years, He left them and went to the Jordan River and received baptism, which baptism, indeed, was not necessary for Him, but He accepted it so that through contact with His sacred Body, there might be communicated to the water the regenerative power for saving those believing and obeying Him.

And this the priest symbolizes when he washes his fingers, not because of necessity, since he is pure in conscience through sacramental confession and clean by a natural bath, but to commemorate the testimony of humility which Jesus Christ gave those wishing to be baptized.

10. The tenth work which our Savior did in this world was that, according to Luke, Mark, and Matthew, after the baptism, He went into the desert and fasted forty days and forty nights, neither eating nor drinking, but the whole time staying in prayer, not praying for Himself but for us.

And this is symbolized when the priest at the middle of the altar bows profoundly and says, "In a spirit of humility . . . ," praying that in the Holy Sacrifice we might become a sacrifice [*hostia*] which is pleasing to the Lord our God.[2] This prayer commemorates the prostrations and humiliations which the Savior was doing in the desert, praying and beseeching. The priest, however, turns to the people saying, "Pray brethren . . . ," for me that my sacrifice and yours may be acceptable before God." And those attending should then say, "The Holy Spirit come over you . . . ."[3] Note that the prayer of Jesus Christ in the desert was secret; so in this step, the priest prays secretly so that not even the deacon or the subdeacon can hear.

11. The eleventh work which Jesus the Savior did was that, after He had fasted, He began to preach, crying out: "Do penance, for the kingdom of God is at hand."

And the priest symbolizes this by saying in a loud voice, "Lift up your hearts."[4] teaching us that Jesus Christ taught both by mouth and by example. And so, as he sings the Preface he holds his hands up, and not down [*elevatas et not demissas*].

12. The twelfth work which Jesus Christ did in this world was that not only was He teaching by word and deed, but He confirmed His sacred teachings with miracles. For only God can work such things—namely, raise the dead, give sight to the blind, heal the paralytics.

And this the priest commemorates when he says three times, "Holy," denoting that Jesus Christ worked miracles not through His human power, but in virtue of the three divine persons, the Father, and the Son, and the Holy Spirit, of one all-powerful God. Finally, he says, *Hosanna*, that is "Saving," to demonstrate that Christ worked miracles so that He might save us.[5]

13. The thirteenth work which He did in this world was when, after He had preached and worked many miracles, at thirty-three years of age, He came to Jerusalem so that He might dine with His disciples. And secretly many things were necessary for the redemption of mankind, especially two, namely the institution of the Most Blessed Sacrament of the Altar and the great sermon which is prolonged in St. John, from chapter thirteen to chapter seventeen.

And this is symbolized when the priest quietly reads the Canon, only the deacon hearing, just as only the apostles heard the sermon of Christ.

14. The fourteenth work was when, these two things done, He entered into the garden [to] Jericho, and there offered three prayers, demonstrating that as man He prayed to God the Father for three conditions of persons—namely, for the holy fathers who were in

purgatory, for those present in the world at that time, and for those in the future. After the third prayer He sweat Blood, warning that those who were to come ought to pray with special fervor because of the great dangers and trials which will shortly come upon them and which they will not be able to overcome unless by fervid prayers and in the strength of patience.

The priest symbolizes these three prayers by making three signs of the cross over the chalice, saying, "Blessed, ascribed, ratified . . . ," and finally two other crosses, of which one over the chalice saying "And of the Blood," that we might know that in His Passion He prayed for Himself insofar as He was a man, and for us sinners.[6]

15. The fifteenth work was when, after the aforesaid prayer, a great multitude of people came forward with a great clamor, with swords and clubs, to seize Jesus. And He was calmly [benevolenter] willing to be seized and bound and led before Pilate, who sentenced Him to death on the cross: from which sentence He wished not to appeal, but gently assumed and carried His blessed cross.

And this is represented in the Mass when the priest takes the host to consecrate it, which he holds in his hands, saying, "And lifting up His eyes to heaven," etc.[7] And then there is a great sounding of bells and of the bell wheel [rotae], signifying the tumult and sounds of the Jews when they arrested Jesus.[8] Then the priest makes the sign of the cross over the host saying, "Bless and break," etc., signifying the sentence of death passed by Pilate.

16. The sixteenth work was when, sentenced to death, Jesus Christ was led to death on Calvary, and there He was crucified between two thieves, one on His right, who is called Dismas, the other on the left, named Gestas.

And this is signified when the priest elevates the Host in which is Christ, God and man, and he holds it with both hands. The right signifies the good thief, the left the bad. After this he elevates the chalice, signifying that Jesus Christ on the cross offered and sacrificed His precious Blood to God the Father for the redemption of mankind. For which reason the priest, elevating the Precious Blood, ought to say to himself, "We offer to You Lord the inestimable price of our redemption."

17. The seventeenth work which Jesus Christ did was that when He was crucified, He did not cease praying. And first, He said in a loud voice, "*Eli! Eli! Lamma sabachtani*"—"My God, My God, why have You abandoned me" (Matt. 27:46), to which words St. Jerome adds: "Look on me." And He continued prayer up to the verse: "Into Your hands I commend My spirit" (Psalms 30:6). And there were 150 verses: Christ on the Cross said as many verses as there are psalms.

And while He was on the cross, the wicked Jews did not cease laying on Him injuries and curses, and others, saying, "Vah, You Who destroy the temple of God," etc. (Matt. 27:40). Others: "If You be the Son of God, come down from the cross." Others, finally, "He saved others;

Himself He cannot save," (Matt. 27:42). And the Lord calmly did not reply but continued in prayer with great patience.

And this the priest symbolizes when, holding his arms extended in the form of a cross, he prays saying, "Mindful, therefore, Lord, we, Your ministers," etc.[9]

18. The eighteenth work which Jesus Christ did in this world was when, although already wounded with four wounds, namely in His hands and feet, nevertheless He wished, after His death, to be pierced with a lance in His sacred side, whence flowed Blood and water. Which miraculously happened, contrary to nature, for all His Blood had already been poured out, first in the scourging, then in the crowning of thorns and in the nailing of His hands and feet.

And these five principal wounds are signified when the priest makes the sign of the cross five times over the Host and Precious Blood saying, "Through Him, and with Him," etc.[10]

19. The nineteenth work was when Christ crucified, crying out, said the seven [last] words, which is commemorated when the priest recites the *Our Father*, in which seven petitions are contained. And, indeed, he does not say it secretly, but singing, just as Christ on the cross spoke out with a loud voice.

20. The twentieth work was that Christ wanted His most sacred humanity to be divided in three parts; namely, the Body on the cross, the Blood shed in the

tortures, and the soul which descended to hell to the holy fathers.

And this is represented in the Mass when the priest divides the Host in three parts. It must be noted, however, that he holds them together because, even though the most holy humanity of Christ had been divided, never was the divinity separated from it; moreover it was united to each part, as St. Paul says: "What He assumed once, He never divided" It is similar to when a fragment of crystal is exposed to the sun and then it is smashed into many more fragments; the sun lights up each part in the same way that it lights up the whole crystal; so each part of the humanity of Christ was personally and substantially filled with the divinity, just as the fragment of crystal is filled with the sun.

21. The twenty-first work which Christ performed was when He converted many kinds of persons, wishing to show the fruit of His passion. And first, He converted the thief, a man of bad life and wicked deeds; second, a centurion, a leader of soldiers who said, "Indeed this man was the son of God" (Mark 15:39); and third, ordinary people, according to which St. Luke said, "And all the multitude of them . . . saw the things that were done," namely the miracles which happened, "returned striking their breasts" (Luke 23:48).

These various persons are symbolized in the Mass when the priest says three times "Lamb of God,"[11] first, for every sinner, signifying that the Lord our God wishes to spare him just as He spared the thief; second, signifying that just as Jesus Christ illuminated the centurion, so the governors of the people, whether spiritual or temporal He desires to illuminate them and to pardon them. And just as souls moved by the passion of Christ come to salvation, so the priest, saying the third Lamb of God, asks on behalf of the whole Christian people that the Lord deign to keep them in peace and in health, to pardon the sins of each, and to make them worthy participants of His holy grace.

22. The twenty-second work which Christ does in this world, was that He did not immediately ascend into heaven after His holy passion, but through His most profound humanity, wished first to descend secretly to hell, that He might give glory to the holy fathers, awaiting with great expectation. At the moment they saw Him, they were filled with great exultation, enjoying essential glory, now and forever free from any pain.

And this the priest prefigures when he puts a particle of the Host into the chalice to denote how the soul of Christ descending to hell so rejoiced the holy fathers and confirmed them, that they hardly knew what happened to them in experiencing such a fullness of happiness. And from that sweetness and love they praised God saying, "Blessed be the Lord God of Israel; because he hath visited and wrought the redemption of his people" (Luke 1:68 [DRV]).

23. The twenty-third work which Jesus Christ did in this world was when, after His painful death, He willed and ordered His Body to be taken down from the cross

by His friends, Joseph of Arimathea, Nicodemus, and Gamaliel, having received permission from Pilate, and they laid Him to rest behind a large stone, which can still be seen today in the Church of the Holy Sepulcher. And then the Virgin Mary and Mary Magdalen and the other devout persons let out great cries of grief.

And this is represented in the Mass when the priest, having given the sign of peace,[12] for a short period of time during which he held the Body of Christ in His hands, ought to think of the sorrow of the Virgin Mary and of the others who were mourning, and so should shed many tears, and conceive a special sorrow for his sins.

24. The twenty-fourth work was that Christ wished to be anointed with balsam and myrrh, to be wrapped in a clean burial cloth, and placed into a tomb newly carved in the stone, without any corruption or fracture.

And this is represented in the Mass when the priest takes the Body of Christ, because the heart of the priest ought to be a new tomb, without corruption; and just as the tomb of Christ was of solid rock, so should he be strong in faith and a good life. And just as the Body of Christ was wrapped in a clean shroud, so the conscience of the priest ought to be cleaned and shine forth with chastity. And just as the Body of Christ was anointed with balsam and spices, so the heart of the priest ought to be saturated with every kind of virtue. And it is fitting that not only the priest but also every Christian should nourish his devotion with these thoughts whilst hearing Mass.

25. The twenty-fifth work which Christ did was when He rose on the third day from death to life, and His tomb was opened.

And this the priest prefigures coming from the middle to the side of the altar, signifying that Christ passed from the mortal world into immortal life. And showing the empty chalice, it signifies the open tomb, and Christ through His infinite power to have risen. And the deacon folds the corporal, in remembrance that the holy shroud, in which the sacred Body of Jesus was wrapped, had been found in the tomb.

26. The twenty-sixth work was that after His resurrection, Christ appeared to the glorious Virgin Mary His mother, although in the Gospel there is no mention of this; but the holy doctors expressly affirm it, and especially St. Ambrose in his book *On Virgins*. And indeed, it was exquisitely fitting that Christ, before any others, visited and comforted His Mother, who more than others had suffered from His death.

And this the priest signifies by saying, with his face to the people, "The Lord be with you."[13] And then he reads the Postcommunion, which is a prayer of great consolation, representing the consoling words which Christ said to His Mother, and the great praise which the holy fathers gave to her saying, "Queen of heaven rejoice," etc.[14]

27. The twenty-seventh work which Christ did in this world was when He appeared to the apostles together in the upper room and said, "Peace be with you."

And this is represented in the Mass when the priest turning around to the people saying again, "The Lord be with you," which is the same as namely peace be with you all.[15]

28. The twenty-eighth work was when He gathered the apostles and said, "Go ye into the whole world, and preach . . ." (Mark 16:15 [DRV]).

And this is symbolized at Mass when the priest says: "Go, the Mass is ended," every believer returning to his work, because the holy sacrifice is completed.

29. The twenty-ninth work was when He fulfilled the promise made to Peter and the holy apostles, namely, establishing St. Peter in possession of the papacy, saying, "Feed My lambs" (John 21:15, 16). Then, indeed, according to all the teachers, He truly constituted him as the head of the universal Church. And to the other apostles He said, "Receive the Holy Spirit; whose sins you forgive," etc. (John 20:22–23), giving them the power of forgiving sins, which is divine power.

And this is represented at the end of Mass when the priest, humbling himself profoundly, bows his head as much as he can before the altar and says, "May it be pleasing to You Blessed Trinity . . . ," petitioning the Trinity that the Holy Sacrifice be acceptable to God and be beneficial for all the people.[16] And this bow which he makes kissing the altar denotes the infinite mercy of our God, Who did not consider it unworthy to humble His divine power, passing on to sinful men the power of forgiving sins. And finally He makes the sign of the cross over the people, signifying that their sins are forgiven though the sacred passion of Christ.

30. The thirtieth and last work of Christ in this world was when, in the presence of His Mother and the holy apostles and more than 500 people, according to St. Paul, standing on the Mount of Olives, He wished to ascend to heaven. And raising His hands He blessed all those who were lamenting His absence, and He returned to where He had come from.

And this is signified in the Mass when the priest, having given the blessing, returns to the sacristy whence he had come.

And so the whole life of our Redeemer is covered in the sacred holy sacrifice of the Mass. To which glory may He lead us, He Who lives and reigns forever and ever. Amen.

Endnotes

1. Fourth work.

(The Priest inaudibly says the following while going to the Altar:)

P. Aufer a nobis, quaesumus, Domine, iniquitates nostras: ut ad Sancta sanctorum puris mereamur mentibus introire. Per Christum Dominum nostrum. Amen.	P. Take away from us, O Lord, we beseech You, our iniquities, that we may enter with pure minds into the Holy of Holies. Through Christ our Lord. Amen.

(He kisses the altar at the place where the saint's relics are enclosed and says:)

P. Oramus te, Domine, per merita Sanctorum tuorum, quorum reliquiae hic sunt, et omnium Sanctorum: ut indulgere digneris omnia peccata mea. Amen.	P. We beseech You, O Lord, by the merits of Your Saints whose relics lie here, and of all the Saints, deign in Your mercy to pardon me all my sins. Amen.

2. Tenth work.

P. In spiritu humilitatis, et in animo contrito suscipiamur a te, Domine: et sic fiat sacrificium nostrum in conspectu tuo hodie, ut placeat tibi, Domine Deus.

P. In a humble spirit and with a contrite heart, may we be accepted by You, O Lord, and may our sacrifice be so offered in Your sight this day as to please You, O Lord God.

3. Tenth work.

(He turns to the congregation and calls on them to join their prayers with his:)

P. Orate fratres: ut meum ac vestrum sacrificium acceptabile fiat apud Deum Patrem omnipotentem.

P. Pray brethren, that my Sacrifice and yours may be acceptable to God the Father Almighty.

S. Suscipiat Dominus sacrificium de manibus tuis ad laudem et gloriam nominis sui, ad utilitatem quoque nostram, totiusque Ecclesiae suae sanctae.

S. May the Lord receive the Sacrifice from your hands to the praise and glory of His Name, for our good, and that of all His holy Church.

4. Eleventh work.

P. Dominus vobiscum.
S. Et cum spiritu tuo.

P. Sursum corda.
S. Habemus ad Dominum.
P. Gratias agamus Domino Deo nostro.
S. Dignum et justum est.

P. May the Lord be with you.
S. And with your spirit.

P. Lift up your hearts.
S. We have lifted them up to the Lord.
P. Let us give thanks to the Lord our God.
S. It is right and just.

5. Twelfth work

Sanctus

(Sung as the Priest begins the Canon. The prayers of the Canon are said in a low voice.)

S/C. Sanctus, Sanctus, Sanctus, Dominus Deus Sabaoth. Pleni sunt coeli, et terra gloria tua. Hosanna in excelsis. Benedictus qui venit in nomine Domini. Hosanna in excelsis.

S/C. Holy, Holy, Holy Lord God of Hosts. Heaven and earth are filled with Your glory. Hosanna in the highest. Blessed is He Who comes in the Name of the Lord. Hosanna in the highest.

6. Fourteenth work.

P. Quam oblationem tu, Deus, in omnibus, quaesumus, benedictam, adscriptam, ratam, rationabilem, acceptabilemque facere digneris: ut nobis Corpus, et Sanguis fiat dilectissimi Filii tui Domini nostri Jesu Christi.	P. O God, deign to bless ✠ what we offer, and make it approved, ✠ effective, ✠ right, and wholly pleasing in every way, that it may become for our good, the Body ✠ and Blood ✠ of Your dearly beloved Son, Our Lord Jesus Christ.

7. Fifteenth work.

The Consecration

P. Qui pridie quam pateretur, accepit panem in sanctas ac venerabiles manus suas, et elevatis oculis in coelum ad te Deum Patrem suum omnipotentem, tibi gratias agens, benedixit, fregit, deditque discipulis suis, dicens: Accipite, et manducate ex hoc omnes.	P. Who, the day before He suffered, took bread into His holy and venerable hands, and having raised His eyes to heaven to You, God, His Almighty Father, giving thanks to You, He blessed ✠ it, broke it, and gave it to His disciples, saying: "Take and eat of this, all of you,
HOC EST ENIM CORPUS MEUM.	FOR THIS IS MY BODY."

8. Fifteenth work.

A footnote in Pere Fages biography has: "You should know that in Spain besides the little bell and the handbell group, there is a wheel armed with bells suspended on the wall, which, when vigorously agitated produces indeed a great commotion [*gran broigt*]."
P. 16, n. 1.

9. Seventeenth work.

P. Unde et memores, Domine, nos servi tui, sed et plebs tua sancta, ejusdem Christi Filii tui Domini nostri tam beatae passionis, nec non et ab inferis resurrectionis, sed et in coelos gloriosae ascensionis: offerimus praeclarae majestati tuae de tuis donis ac datis, hostiam puram, hostiam sanctam, hostiam immaculatam, Panem sanctum vitae aeternae, et Calicem salutis perpetuae.

P. Mindful, therefore, Lord, we, Your ministers, as also Your holy people, of the same Christ, Your Son, Our Lord, remember His blessed passion, and also of His resurrection from the dead, and finally of His glorious ascension into heaven, offer to Your supreme Majesty, of the gifts bestowed upon us, the pure ✛ Victim, the holy ✛ Victim, the all-perfect ✛ Victim: the holy ✛ Bread of life eternal and the Chalice ✛ of perpetual salvation.

10. Eighteenth work.

P. Per quem haec omnia, Domine, semper bona creas, sanctificas, vivificas, benedicis, et praestas nobis.

P. Through Whom, Lord, You always create, sanctify, ✛ fill with life, ✛ bless ✛ and bestow upon us all these good things.

11. Twenty-first work.

Agnus Dei
(Sung during the Priest's preparation for Communion.)

C. Agnus Dei, qui tollis peccata mundi, miserere nobis. Agnus Dei, qui tollis peccata mundi, miserere nobis. Agnus Dei, qui tollis peccata mundi, dona nobis pacem.

C. Lamb of God, Who take away the sins of the world, have mercy on us. Lamb of God, Who take away the sins of the world, have mercy on us. Lamb of God, Who take away the sins of the world, grant us peace.

12. The twenty-third work.

The Peace

P. Pax Domini sit semper vobiscum.	P. May the peace ✛ of the Lord be ✛ always with ✛ you.
S. Et cum spiritu tuo.	S. And with your spirit.

13. Twenty-sixth work.

Postcommunion
(Stand.)

P. Dominus vobiscum.	P. May the Lord be with you.
S. Et cum spiritu tuo.	S. And with your spirit.
P. Oremus.	P. Let us pray.

(Here he says the Postcommunion Prayer.)

S. Amen.   S. Amen.

14. Twenty-sixth work.

Regina caeli

V. Regina caeli, laetare, alleluia.
R. Quia quem meruisti portare, alleluia.

V. Resurrexit, sicut dixit, alleluia.
R. Ora pro nobis Deum, alleluia.
V. Gaude et laetare, Virgo Maria, alleluia.
R. Quia surrexit Dominus vere, alleluia.

Queen of Heaven

V. Queen of Heaven, rejoice, alleluia.
R. For He Whom you did merit to bear, alleluia.

V. Has risen as He said, alleluia.
R. Pray for us to God, alleluia.
V. Rejoice and be glad, O Virgin Mary, alleluia.
R. For the Lord has truly risen, alleluia.

15. Twenty-seventh work.

Final Prayer and Dismissal

P. Dominus vobiscum.
S. Et cum spiritu tuo.

P. Ite, Missa est.
S. Deo gratias.

P. May the Lord be with you.
S. And with your spirit
D. Go, you are sent forth.
S. Thanks be to God.

16. Twenty-ninth work.

(The celebrant prays in a low voice.)

P. Placeat tibi, sancta Trinitas, obsequium servitutis meae: et praesta; ut sacrificium, quod oculis tuae majestatis indignus obtuli, tibi sit acceptabile, mihique, et omnibus, pro quibus illud obtuli, sit, te miserante, propitiabile. Per Christum Dominum nostrum. Amen.

P. May the tribute of my worship be pleasing to You, most Holy Trinity, and grant that the sacrifice which I, all unworthy, have offered in the presence of Your Majesty, may be acceptable to You, and, through Your mercy, obtain forgiveness for me and all for whom I have offered it. Through Christ Our Lord. Amen.

P. Benedicat vos omnipotens Deus, Pater, et Filius, et Spiritus Sanctus.
S. Amen.

P. May Almighty God bless you, the Father, and the Son, ✢ and the Holy Spirit.
S. Amen.

the penguin pocket book of
travel
tips

Other books in the Penguin Pocket Series

THE AUSTRALIAN CALORIE COUNTER
THE AUSTRALIAN EASY SPELLER
AUSTRALIAN GARDENING CALENDAR
CASSEROLES FOR FAMILY AND FRIENDS
CHAIRING AND RUNNING MEETINGS
CHESS MADE EASY
CHOOSING A NAME FOR YOUR BABY
CHOOSING AUSTRALIAN WINES
THE COMPACT GUIDE TO WRITING LETTERS
FAMILY FIRST AID
GABRIEL GATÉ'S FAST PASTA
GABRIEL GATÉ'S FAVOURITE FAST RECIPES
GABRIEL GATÉ'S ONE-DISH DINNERS
GOOD FOOD FOR BABIES AND TODDLERS
HOW TO MAKE OVER 200 COCKTAILS
HOW TO PLAY MAH JONG
HOW TO SELL ANYTHING BY SOMEONE WHO HAS
JULIE STAFFORD'S FAT, FIBRE AND ENERGY COUNTER
JULIE STAFFORD'S JUICING BOOK
MICROWAVE MEALS IN MINUTES
MICROWAVE TIPS AND TECHNIQUES
THE PENGUIN POCKET BOOK OF ETIQUETTE
THE PENGUIN POCKET BOOK OF QUOTATIONS
PLAYING CASINO GAMES TO WIN
THE POCKET AUSSIE FACT BOOK
THE POCKET CAKES AND PUDDINGS COOKBOOK
THE POCKET MUFFIN BOOK
THE POCKET WOK COOKBOOK
THE POCKET SOUP COOKBOOK
REMOVING STAINS
SPEAKING IN PUBLIC
TRAINING YOUR MEMORY
USING YOUR NOODLES
WEDDING ETIQUETTE
YOUR NEW BABY